With Respect to Wings

poetry by Donella Dornwell McLean

TRANSCENDENT ZERO PRESS
HOUSTON, TEXAS

Copyright © 2024 by Donella Dornwell McLean.

Contents of this publication remain the intellectual property of Donella Dornwell McLean. None of these works may be reproduced in any format, whether electronically or in print, without consent from the publisher Transcendent Zero Press or Donella Dornwell McLean except as portions in reviews.

Cover design: AJ Price Design

Publisher contact: Editor@transcendentzeropress.org

ISBN: 978-1-946460-59-2

With Respect to Wings

poetry by Donella Dornwell McLean

*"From cocoon forth a butterfly
As lady from her door
Emerged – a summer afternoon –
Repairing everywhere ..."*

Emily Dickinson

Dedication

To my baby brother, James,

who's always been a great support to me

Table of Contents

Life Isn't Candy Land / 7
A Feminist's Favor / 9
In the Shadow of Never / 10
Happy Insanity / 11
A Sigh at the Beach / 12
The Holy Spirit Butterfly / 13
Visiting the Nursing Home / 14
An Ode to a Red Elegy / 15
Saunter Like a Woman / 16
Thoughts Invade Me Like an Axe / 17
Drop the Ball / 18
Bird Marrow / 19
A Prayer / 20
Twilight Looms / 21
Blowing Out a Candle / 22
Carrion / 23
a hesitation / 24
Little Free / 25
Slow grade down a windy hill / 26
Pinnacle of us / 27
Riding a see saw alone...is / 28
Normal is a misnomer / 29
I'll Fly Away / 30
Butterfly Fodder / 31
The Key / 32
Rise up, hope! / 33
From the Mouth of an Angel / 34
With Respect to Wings / 35
Laura, the Parrot / 36
The Light of Love / 37
Confetti Letters / 38
A Visit / 39
Fly By Me / 40
Dreams of Flight / 41
Ballet dancer / 42
I've built a rapport / 43
Resilient? / 44

This Mess / 45
Baby Brother / 46
Starry Night / 47
Lantana Bush in My Yard / 48
To: Johnny Marr / 49
What came of the day I was taken to the psyche ward / 50
Transcending the Cold / 51
Meet me from / 52
the subject of this piece / 53
Remember / 54
I Need the Wings to Help Me Heal / 55
grasping at straws this / 56
orange butterfly flits / 57
Acknowledgements / 58
Bio / 59

Life Isn't Candy Land

Life isn't Candy Land.
It's not Barbie and Ken
Holding hands with
Plum Fairy guiding
The way to
California
Ocean Beach
Bliss.

Life isn't a serenade.
Love isn't flowers
On Valentine's Day.
Love is being there
When everyone else
Has gone away.

Life is love but
Candy, well candy
I can have every day.

But it's not so easy
To find love.

So here's to chocolate
For the lonely and
For those who Love
Hasn't met lately.
For those who've
Never and never shall
Feel so much

Love, the Elusive,
Is gathered like
Pleats behind
The stage curtain
Waiting for opening night.

Love is holding
Your only baby,
Knowing you'll
Never have another–
The pleasure and pain,
The happiness and regret.
What's left?
To live and live well
With pleats in my hand,
Candy in my pocket,
And baby girl singing
With me to the radio,
As we drive
Down roads not knowing,
Not knowing,
Not knowing,
Where we are going.

                                          April 9, 2012

A Feminist's Favor

A feminist's favor
Is a glimpse at forever
And how mighty the lady
Has Fallen...so far
And handed her regard
Like a stalwart wind
Answer to begin
A moment in the midst
The question is when
Find our tomorrows
Is archaically demure?
When proclaim is the name
Ready for remembrance
A strong gust forward once more.

In the Shadow of Never

What is the matter with this craver?
Why must she savor so?
But now she runs from the flavor.
When will the happiness glow?
In the shadow of never
She will find him there.

Happy Insanity

A train trembled by
My hand holding
Four year old hers
As hands vibrated,
We walked in a hide away
Park in Austin
Edgy and exhausted,
Anxious and aching
To hold your hand, too.

Take mine, lead me
To an alternative,
Happy insanity,

The kind where
A touch cures
And a laugh
Tangles my legs
In yours in bed,
Closer than caresses

And the definition
Of crazy
Doesn't exist:

Heaven in my
Hands.

February 17, 2012

A Sigh at the Beach

An ocean breeze
A modicum of air
That translates the rush
Of a moment into a
Stream full of waves like
The locks of your hair,

You can't get away from
The movement
Even though the stirrings
Aren't visible

(briny retreat makes the
Beach replete
With salty tasting air.)

The Holy Spirit Butterfly

Oh butterfly
Fly by me
Oh butterfly
You remind me
Of my sister
Oh butterfly
Thanks for the remember
Of that wretched September

Oh butterfly
Guide me to her
She needs rest
And the gravesite
Doesn't serve her best

Oh butterfly
You exude her soul
In every wing beat
Oh butterfly
Thanks for the remember

Visiting the Nursing Home

My mom babysat
While I slept
In her urine laden
Hospital bed in
A Medicaid nursing home
For 45 minutes when
Sleep was so brand new

My four year old newly out
Of napping, me working nights
And on the verge of losing
My mind for the first time
Among many times then

Waking to guest trays
Of runny slop–putrid smells adrift
My daughter giggling
As her grandma Della
Followed behind her in
A wheelchair–moving
Her legs but unable to
Bear weight. I tried
To drown out the
Laughter for a few
Doses of slumber,
Only to face mania-driven
Mind warp in my wake.

An Ode to a Red Elegy

Fly by me cardinals
Red male, pinkish female
You glint in the trees like a gem
Twinkling in the air
Rubies with wings,
Feathered features,
Furrowed fowl

Picking at the ground
Making a meal out of
Measly morsels you just found
Pecking at the branches
Beneath your wings

You are a stand-in for my sister
Lost to homelessness–a visit
With each encounter with you
Brings a memory of her–
an elegy in sight–an ode
In measure

Saunter Like a Woman

Saunter like a woman
Sway back and forth
High heels, low heels, flats
Klink, klink of a shoe
Is the klink, klink of a glass
Message to anyone watching
She's going to move with purpose
And it's not just the
Child-birthing hips
The legs are a symphony
Moving in time to the
Instrument of smooth rhythm
That's a walk on salty sand
Deep dip in crystal waters
Walk aways out then swim
Because like water, she moves
Like ocean waves

Thoughts Invade Me Like an Axe

Thoughts invade me like an axe
Chip, chip in kind
Dark, darker still
The axe timbers my will
To think a thought
Could tether and hold
Like horse's reins:
Direct me to better days.

Drop the Ball

Drop the ball
Pick it back up

Drop it again
Pick it back up

These are the occurrences
Of sometimes love

A moment then nothing,
A moment then years gone by,
A moment for a lifetime

So much depends on moments
Too much of nothing

In between to rectify the sorrow
To emulsify the memory

Bird Marrow

Laughing comes harder
With a hardened heart

Mine is marble
Too little to consume
There's no sustenance
Birdseed specks
Of love left to falter

When once there was
Marrow now bone
Is depleted of all
Red blood cells–cut
To tomorrow–the end
Of today–the beginning
Of new life

May my laughter emerge
On a brand new stage!

A Prayer

Steward of kindness
I give in to your mercy
Grant me peace, Dear Lord
Make the mountains morsels
Remedied in your mystery

Thank you for love
Even if I never know
Another kindred soul
Thanks for those I have
Known before

Help me remember others
First, dear steward.

I want to help them
Like so many have helped
Me in life.
Life is so short–make mine full
Of life and vibrant wonder.

Amen.

Twilight Looms

Twilight looms
A moon askew
Claim the night
Drift into a morning glow
Somehow I'll never know
Where all the time goes

Twilight looms
A moon anew
Bright shine the night glows
Shake the stars
Make them stay
Until dawn breaks

Blowing Out a Candle

You blow out a candle and
The smoke wafts away like
A butterfly caught in the wind
This way and that way
Swirling until it dissipates
Into simply an aroma in the air
But in gray overtones

You get so caught up in the
Movement of the air that the
Smoke fades in wafty current
Spirals–a salutation to your nose
Palatable like cigarette remains;
A teensy butt preserved as a memory

Carrion

I am nothing more
a corpse in mummy form
the remains of a woman
tattered in my seams
crows and vultures gather
for a taste of flesh...to the marrow
of the matter...watch the
blood spatter...have I satisfied
the hungriest of birds that
have flown away?

April 4, 2024

a hesitation
a movement
of muscle
a moment
these are what
we are made of

I can't take back
all I felt
I can't calm
my young self
I want to shovel
a piece of me away

save her for
another day
a sentiment
a treasure
Please make
it better

give a piece
on a platter
of measure
Thank you, God
for the remember

October 17, 2021

Little Free

Big sister little free
Fun sister down on me
Unmedicated sister
Such a disease
Give in to pressure
Then no release

I can't help her
Help herself
And she's in it:
This oppression
This constant defiance
Denial in overdrive
Then lapse into death

We'll never know
How or when
But we miss you sister...
Your remarkable smile
The unselfish ornament

If I could hug you
And say I love you
For the many
Ways you've given
And not received.

May 20, 2020

Slow grade down a windy hill
Transforms into vast ruptures
Of mealy emotion...I'm not myself
When I don't sleep...sleep evades me and
Lack of sleep erodes my
Soul. Could all this anxiety be my downfall?
Record breaking lip biting. Once more I'm
Tainted by the past. It oozes from my pores.
Causes colossal disorder where once there
Was joy.

                                                April 3, 2021

Pinnacle of us
Brought down to the core
Minuscule type memories
I'd trade you for pain
For that's all that's left.

Open the fissure
Of unbridled sorrow
Add a tidbit of joy
Close down the misery

Explode all the happiness
Make a new mold
Bring on tomorrows
Let's see who emerges
Out of the fire

Be it human or phoenix
I welcome a new strength.
Ashes mixed with molten
Soon to be molten no more
And joy is the tragedy

Riding a see saw alone...is impossible...empty shell of metal...zero weight to lift me...solace...in knowing we are all alone...the see saw is a rock...skipping rocks across a vast ocean of time...and then the submergence...accelerated speed...dipping deeper...to the ground beneath the water– A final resting place.

January 24, 2021

Normal is a misnomer
A skeleton before
Messy skin and blood
Are piled on

Courage to face
Abnormal
Streams through
My veins

Ghost town of sorrows
Wake me up tomorrow
A kiss on the lips
Doesn't bode well
For these remnants
Of "normal" physical
Displays

Surely remembrance
Of sustenance
Is sustenance enough
Just like remembrance
Of a kiss is pleasantry
Enough

September 8, 2020

I'll Fly Away

The flutter of butterfly wings

Is like the flutter of a heartbeat
Ring true
New ring
In the laughter of my sister's voice

A voice I won't forget too soon:
Deep and distinct
Eager and longing

I'll never get to hug her again
Relinquish my grasp
Let Jesus hold her instead
She's not ours,
She's His

Whole and pure
Broken no more
We shed tears
But she is laughing
In Heaven.

May 11, 2020

Butterfly Fodder

When you drive
In Bastrop in Spring
There are always butterflies
Stuck to your car grill:
So much butterfly fodder
And all I can think
Of is Charity as she
Is now reminiscent in butterfly form
At every turn
Making moment of air
Flitting at the earth
That couldn't handle her
The sweet selflessness of her
The solitude that's left is
Unquenchable
That miracle in the making
Of a kind sister

April 2024

The Key

The remainder of sorrow
Keeps me grounded
In hope for tomorrows

Joy has eluded
Me-hid behind
Bookshelves of every
Room I've rented

That gave me insight
Into insanity when
She was peering out
I became tackled
By turmoil, the unrequited love
Caught up with me

And twisted me into a
Keyhole of a person...
The door closed shut, locked
Out the love, locked
In the darkness-cinch
Some more-pinch
With the door-the key
Was always missing-that
Remedy-the elixir to turn
Him into mine,
To turn me into Joy.

Rise up, hope!

Rise up, hope
The eternal height of my existence
Like hoping you'd love me back

Rise up, hope
The masqueraded fear
The "courage" that doesn't cower

Rise up, hope
The barrels are mostly empty,
Soon to be filled.

Rise up, hope
A testament to the many
That God is real

Rise up, hope
For those who believe
He is Risen!

March 10, 2024

From the Mouth of an Angel

Now that I can fly
I can climb the highest tree
And meet you in the middle
And meet you in between

With these wings that I've acquired
I can finally become what
They didn't see in me on earth
I was a little skewed there
Not so much air-full of fluff

With this newfound title
I could've flown all over the world
But I'm hovering by your door

I have a duty to watch over
The sister I left behind
And now I'm not sorry
For God is my guide

Now that I'm gone from earth
I've earned these angelic wings
To keep me afloat–to keep her flying free.

With Respect to Wings

Butterflies have them
So do birds
Some insects do
And angels too

I want to grasp
A couple of wings
And make them mine
So I can fly by
Those I've left behind

Silver essence
In gilded night
The epitome of solace
The accompaniment of grief
The delivery of comfort
These wings are a vehicle

Like no other
The movement of air
The moment of care
a visit from a winged one
could cure the sorrow
but it offers a tomorrow
where once we weren't
so sure

Laura, the Parrot

Gallant green with jaunting yellow
And pristine blue
She was a beauty
She would make her calls
Her freedom clipped
Like her wings
A mystery to see her fly
Never happened in the
Year I knew her
I fed her a couple of times
She pecked me each time
With her long, protruding
Beak
Pliers, the grip
Malice, the memory
Manifests
I remember distinctly,
She didn't like crackers.

The Light of Love

Love bites...it's teeth bear down so strong...
All
I'm left with is gristle but still I'm hanging on
Bare bones won't stop me,

Let's elaborate:

Even 100 million man-made sunbeams
Aka lightbulbs
Bear no light against this love

                                      June 22, 2024

Confetti Letters

Ringlets of curves
Among a bed of confetti
I'd send in letters
To him far away overseas,
A reminder that love
Was present–in tiny specks
A hundred times over
Where colors abound

June 25, 2024

A Visit

Dragonfly
Landed on
My purse
Sat there
For 15 minutes
And I didn't
Move an inch

Iridescent he was
And blissful I was,
A visit from another
I think my passed family
Members were saying
Hello and nature
Was waving, too.

A mixture of two worlds...
Synonyms, a treasure...
Antonyms in measure–
Then he fluttered away

July 3, 2024

Fly By Me

The common housefly
Brings no remembrance
Of people from beyond,
It simply leaves you
With a feeling of malaise

Because they are disgusting
These flies make you want to
Bring out the swatter...
No respect of *their* wings

"buzz by me if you dare."

July 12, 2024

Dreams of Flight

We all have dreams
Where we can fly
Our arms become wings
Soaring over the trees
Making a memory as we
Tower over buildings
No fear of heights
In these dreams

Simply conquering
Our physics
How wondrous
To topple no more
To conquer the wind
To traverse the sky
Only to wake at morning's light
In a bed once more

July 12, 2024

Ballet dancer
Sinewy muscle
Firm finesse
Twirling wonder
Stark contrast

Work harder
Even longer
Get to the pointe
Skin to skin contact

Then bleed at the toe
Give into more
I'd like to watch you prance
Can you see me dance?

I've built a rapport
With sleep
Sleep needs me
Sleep deceives me
Sometimes sleep
Evades me
But sleep always
Betrays me
By not delivering
On it's promise
To sway me
Back to sleep
Hush-hush.

Resilient?

Resiliency is in my make-up
From the beginning
I've endured
Flea-infested,
Tick-infested
Home with no electricity

A tragic fire
That burned my brother
Grotesquely
And memory of
Mood altered,
Though devoid
Parents
Who were married and divorced
To each other five times

I picked up this
Habit of discourse
On instability from them

But "they" call me
Resilient only
Because I've survived thus far.

This Mess

Who do I need
To see to find out
Who I can be?

A therapist?
A nurse practitioner?
A psychiatrist?

"Herr Doktor" as Plath said
But I want more

I'm not enough and
Too much all at once

Too much flesh
Not enough finesse

A bed full of meds
Nights full of distress
I can be just this mess.

Baby Brother

A big fellow sure
But more:
A man
Who is a father
To many and loyal
To plenty

A hard worker,
A great example
And loving
And gentle with his girls
When it comes down to it

Just a phone call away,
Talking me through
A tire change at 2 a.m.

Words can't express how
Proud I am of my baby brother–
My confidante–my friend–my hero–
My family

Starry Night

My eyes are tripping
On stars as I stumble
Through the night sky
With only the moon
And their light

I rest my head on the bed
Of night only to find a
Morning dew glistening
In the first light of day–
A travesty to have lost
Another starry night.

Lantana Bush in My Yard

souls of family in
butterfly form visit me
gold, pink blooms await

To: Johnny Marr

Marr Made Music
Manchester Made Marr
Made Morrissey's Music
Make Marr Much More
Make Morrissey Mad
Manchester Made Magnificent Music
Made Music Mine

December 9, 2011

What came of the day I was taken to the psyche ward

I miss him like the droughty land cracks for water.

For I cracked that day when I said, "I love you, I love you, I ...."
To the police officer who'd just handcuffed me.

I thought he was in hell and me in heaven trying to get him back.
We were separated and there was no escape...I would do what I could to make us one...to merge the good and the evil.

But now I know that it was me who was the lost one. I was the one the drugs had to find and make better.
The only place was the psyche ward and it was meant for me.
I was meant to be dosed with Depakote and Risperdal and highly so.
That's what made reality shine through my frontal lobe and display the sad truth:
He didn't want a mental case and what well-bred man would?

So solitude is my only friend, I embrace it, I need it.
It keeps the pain away though when I stop and think
The memories of him are pain enough.

Enough to keep the pills cascading down my throat night after night
But day after day, I miss him...and no psyche ward can cure me now.

May 17, 2007

Transcending the Cold

Like Lot's wife
I look back;
See you there.

Flesh freezes,
Toes tingle,
Socks on my

Hands as gloves
No jacket
To keep me

Warm this time...
The madness
I meet with

Snow and sleet.
Chemicals!
Breathe heavy,

Medicines:
I'm made of
Much, much more.

De-icing
Dissolved salt
And yet a

Pillar of
Pills remains
Sanity!

Meet me from
Yesterday
To today...

Cold can't stay.

May 28, 2011

the subject of this piece

you are the subject
the one who isn't willing

the one who just wants peace

you are the subject
the topic I'll digress to
when everything else is said

or I've had too much to drink

you are the subject
that I read in each poem
the ones of love and such nonsense

yeah I'm lonely...so what
you are the subject

I want to talk of others
but then you have to butt in

don't get me wrong...
you are a welcome distraction

you are the subject
of my life.

August 19, 2008

Remember

I will always remember
Until dementia takes hold

I will always remember
How you listened when no one else would

I will always remember
How fawn made me face my fear

I will always remember
That the love wasn't real

I will always remember
That to me the love is real

I will always remember
That at night I search for you

I will always remember
That's why I can't sleep

July 19, 2024

I Need the Wings to Help Me Heal

All the wings have turned against me
They haunt me like your memories do

I want to remember my family members
But grief can't be on-going

I need a reprieve
I need to see this as positive
I need to see you disappear
So the wings can help me heal

July 19, 2024

grasping at straws this
yellow feeling takes over
should I pick just one?

July 24, 2024

orange butterfly flits
at me like anxiety,
lingering at will

July 24, 2024

Acknowledgements

I would like to thank God for giving me the gift of poetry. It is my medium and I feel called to share with others. Thank you to my beta readers. I appreciate all your input. I appreciate Dustin Pickering for making this manuscript into the book it became. You have always been so supportive. To AJ Price for collaborating with me for the cover art. You are amazing! To my daughter whom I'll always be grateful. To my brother, James and his family...you are my rock and my friend.

DONELLA DORNWELL MCLEAN is a poet through and through. She has a BA in Creative Writing and English. Her other collections are *Answer to My Ellipsis, I've Come Unstirred, Contentions with Joy,* and *Perspirations on Paper.* She has one adult daughter. She lives in Central Texas near family. Donella is a lover of caffeine and cats.

Made in the USA
Coppell, TX
22 November 2024